TREE BREATHING

an approach to meditative wholeness

Simon H. Lilly

ISBN: 9781905454259 (Tree Seer)

INTRODUCTION TO "TREE BREATHING"

This current volume is a new version of Tree Seer Publication's *"Tree Sutras"*, first published in 2004. This new book, *"Tree Breathing"* has full colour images for the first time, combining the symbols of the tree keys with their appropriate colour sequences. To the original text of the tree sutras has been added a complete new level of information, the tree breaths.

A little about Tree Spirit Healing.

Tree spirit healing is a series of processes and techniques that have arisen over many years, initially deriving from work with tree essences, (vibrational, or resonance, medicines made from the flowers of trees). It consists of a range of methods to bring the harmonising field of tree energy into the human energy field. It draws on broadly defined shamanic processes but the primary source of inspiration and information is from the trees themselves. How do trees talk to us? The same way as trees move around from place to place: they encourage by their qualities or their nature other, more mobile species, to act as their vehicles. So, with trees talking: entering into the presence of trees with quietness it is possible to translate that silence, which each tree species shapes, into the frequencies of language that we understand as thought.

Acceptance of this methodology relies upon cultural understanding of reality. In the past (most of the last hundred thousand years) wisdom, information and intelligence was not personally 'owned' as it is today. Self-awareness was awareness of some sort of self-presence embedded in the larger self-presence of the people and the land. Thus, a thought, inspiration, idea was not necessarily owned as original and 'mine', but accepted or rejected as any other sense – as things from the world. Such spiritual ecology deeply favours the philosophy and processes of Buddhism and Taoism, as well as some shamanic systems, and can be found reflected in Tree Spirit Healing.

Tree Spirit Healing, like consciousness and like life itself, is essentially very simple. It is the inter-relationships, the commentaries on their structure and nature, that often becomes complicated. Silence is consciousness. All thought, all language, is a ccommentary upon the nature of silence. The paradox of Tree Spirit Healing is thus to acquire a state of stillness through different types of activity.

The Colour Sequences

The effectiveness of Tree Spirit Healing relies to a large extent on being able to access and activate the deep mind - those areas of awareness beyond the normal levels of language streams and the linearity of cause and effect. The deeper we go within the mind, the more inclusive and universal become the perceptions and understanding. As one dives deep, division, distinction and particularities change their status, becoming far less informing and valuable. They are replaced by a sense of connectivity, reflection and unity. Then the continuous subject-object dialogue of conscious mind-chatter, the I and Non-I, transforms into a more encompassing, global connectivity of being. The subjective is subsumed, transformed or is absorbed by the objective. Inner and outer distinctions become less relevant. The experience takes over from the experiencer.

At these levels, colour becomes one of the most, if not the primary code of meaning. Colour is the broadest of symbolic languages. It is broader than image and shape, broader than sound. Colour plugs into the biology at a cellular and molecular level because it consists of frequencies of light energy that interact with and change the processes and chemical interactions of all physical bodies.

The colours used for each tree key image are thus immediately and profoundly recognised by the deep mind. Each is an energy signature, an equation, an identification sequence that reveals the core manifesting qualities of the tree - how it inwardly and outwardly expresses its patterns of manifestation, and how it unfolds and interacts with the rest of creation.

Teasing out meaning from these colour combinations is not necessary. Explanations are at best only partial commentaries from narrow viewpoints, though it can be a rewarding contemplative and meditative exercise for those who have a broad enough understanding of the multiple, layered correspondences of colours to draw out significances. Like all translations, however, these interpretations necessarily leave out as much as they include, and express limited perspectives.

The deep mind and the body recognises the gestalt of colour sequence for each tree. Paying attention to our instant emotional reaction when we see a series of images reveals very effectively the relationship we have with each of those energy patterns. Three distinct responses are possible: like, dislike and neutrality (attraction, repulsion, indifference). We are either instantly fed and comforted by each colour combination, or disturbed by the colours, or not really affected one way or the other. Indifference indicates that a colour's energy has no bearing on our current internal equilibrium. Attraction, (like or delight) indicates that the energy those colours represent and manifest in some way feed and support our energy state (whether this is a state of true equilibrium and balance or, more typically, a false, temporary, make-do-and-mend, habitual limited, working equilibrium). A colour combination we find displeasing, jarring or upsetting in some way reflects an inability to process that energy pattern. It thus tends to show up fractures and weaknesses within our own personal energy make-up at the time.

So what we can look for is a strong reaction - either positive/like or negative/dislike. These reactions show us the extremes of our energy states. They reveal what maintains and supports, as well as what disrupts and causes change. Colour combinations that we dislike can highlight stresses and imbalances that need addressing in order to begin to approach a more healthy internal equilibrium. Colour combinations that we like, or aesthetically approve of, feed those parts of our energy system that are working pretty well in harmony at that time, or that are well-suited to our current energy requirements.

To avoid confronting energy patterns that we instinctively turn away from will not, in the long run, bring us any benefit. We should be able to process and integrate the whole range of experience in a balanced, supporting way. But it takes more courage and persistence to focus on changing what is not balanced within us than to support our familiar and comfortable habit patterns.

In the end, every tree, no matter what its energy characteristics might be, will bring us to a greater state of balance and harmony, either by supporting us or by challenging us. At different times we need and prefer support, whilst at other times we are happy and willing to encourage a change of state.

It is important to realise that within each choice there are likely to be some qualities that highlight and support our positive goals as well as addressing related imbalances and problems. When the deep mind selects a colour sequence and tree key symbol both easy and difficult issues will be involved at different levels of our experience.

The Tree Key Symbols

The images used here for each tree represent the qualities of energy and life behind the physical form that we ordinarily recognise with our outer senses as this or that species of tree. It is true that the outer form often indicates the characteristics of the inner energy or spirit, (in the same way that we can often tell quite a lot about a person from a photograph), but the visual key enables us to go beyond the habits of the conscious mind, with its preferences to categorise, measure and define.

The physical form of a tree (and of any living being), is like the tip of an iceberg - it shows us that there is, right in this world, but not visible to our normal senses, a greater spiritual being. In our Western culture we tend to accept something as real if it is solid and can be clearly described and measured in some way.

In traditional tribal cultures, physical objects are seen as signs that spiritual beings are present. To a tribal mind 'things' are simply footprints, trails of spiritual beings, shadows of a much more vibrant reality that exists beyond the reach of our ordinary senses.

So each design is a summing up, a translation, a symbolic rendering, of the dance of life of that tree. It is the expression of a tree's unique creativity, of how it manifests and moulds the elements of the universe in its own way.

These images have emerged from particular times set aside for focus and contemplation on each tree. Some images appeared straight away in front of the mind's eye, whilst others took time and effort to cajole into a fixed shape. No doubt there are other images that can represent each tree – in the same way that no two photographs of a dancer in motion will be exactly the same, but nonetheless all will still be records of the same dance. It is, in the end, always limiting to reduce the processes of dynamic life, ever changing and re-inventing itself, to a simple moment of rigid fact.

Tree Breathing

Tree breathing is one of the simplest and most effective of Tree Spirit Healing techniques. It quietens and internalises our awareness quickly and without effort. This makes it a satisfying way to achieve a deep meditative state, especially for those who have found other types of meditation frustrating.

Each tree breath engages the body and the mind. Focus on the physical body naturally takes us away from the habitual thought-processes of ordinary consciousness, not just internal dialogues, but also our emotional involvement, our fears and anxieties.

Whilst our physical breath continues in a relaxed, normal way in and out of our lungs, during tree breathing we imagine that, at the same time, our inbreath and outbreath are being channelled in very specific pathways in and out of the body.
When we place attention on a part of the body with the mind, then particular physical and subtle energetic structures are activated automatically. A tree breath focuses our attention on those areas and structures that are sensitive to the unique qualities of a particular tree species, helping us to harmonise and resonate with the tree's spiritual essence.

Tree breathing is a somatic, body-based, 'feeling' technique that requires no intellectual involvement at all. After a few moments getting the creative imagination used to the flow of the tree breath, we can relax within the experience, allowing thoughts and feelings to come and go without being distracted. If we do sometimes lose focus, it is easy enough to bring our attention back again to the pathways of the in and out breaths as before.

The information presented for each breath is as complete as it is needed to be. If the pathway for the breath is to be precise, then those details are given. For example, if the instruction is to breath in through the feet, then there is no need to be any more precise with your visualisation. If the instruction is to breath through the toes, then that should be clearly imagined. Sometimes the breath is to be imagined following a specific direction through the body until it is exhaled. With other tree breaths the most important thing is the place where the inbreath and outbreath are visualised. In those cases, allow your own creative mind to deduce its own pathways between one point and the other, or simply focus on the given in and out locations.

Tree breathing can be combined with many other Tree Spirit Healing techniques. In this book are presented tree sutra, tree breath, tree key and colour sequences. If it is possible to be in the presence of the actual tree, or to use the flower essence made from the tree, or to hold a piece of the wood of the tree, then this can add another level of contact with the tree's energy.

But each technique is also self-sufficient and effective by itself. It is worth experimenting with each element and process, both separately, simultaneously and in a sequence. For example:
try a few moments visualisation of the colours or gazing at the tree symbol, followed by using the tree breath for a further few minutes. Then relax quietly for a while, paying attention to your internal energetic state (thoughts, sensations, emotions). When you are more familair with the techniques, you may find it easy to do the tree breath at the same time as gazing or visualising.

Tree Sutras

The word 'sutra' comes from the traditions of India and the Himalayas. Literally it means 'stitch' or 'thread', but usually it refers to a saying, statement or verse in sacred texts. (We derive the medical term 'suture', a stitch, from the same root word). The idea of a thread or stitch is something slight, something economical, thin but appropriate with which to join things together, to make links between, to unite, to hold together. So a sutra is a thread of language, a thread of thought, which links together separate, but related, ideas and concepts. Very often, sutras are abbreviations, reminders to those who understand the thread of meaning, who already know the context of the words.

The tree sutras presented here 'stitch together' images and ideas intended to invoke the flavour of how each tree species interacts in a healing way with human beings. They bear a resemblance to magical, gnomic verses, riddles, or even haiku. They are less like explanations and more like music or paintings. Words are pictures. They are shapes that symbolise sounds that signify experiences. Understanding a word requires that you know not only the pronunciation, the sound, but that you can recognise, summon up into your mind the memory, the thought pictures. To spell is to conjure up, to speak is to bring into existence.

Each tree sutra is meant to be evocative, to be able to gather related experiences together in a roundabout way. The meanings, at a conscious level are often ambiguous, even contradictory, but at the deeper levels of the mind – in the unconscious that functions wholly by symbol and feeling – the images create a resonance of experience and understanding.

Our obsessive need for meaning is a dangerous by-product of a rationally-based scientific educational system (itself the product of a society that requires 'usefulness' of all its members). 'Meaning' in this instance is not so much 'understanding' or 'seeing', as simply being able to fit an experience or concept into a pre-existent pattern that has been chosen to define the world and how it works, (the consensus view). With this bias for 'making sense' of things, any experience that cannot be placed within the scheme satisfactorily gets dismissed, ignored or ridiculed. It becomes unreal – no matter how tangible the experience. Interesting phenomena simply become invisible to science and to the 'real world', even when they are in plain view, just because they seem to distort or modify the accepted pattern too much.

Being brought up in such a climate creates the tendency to want to know what everything 'means'. What is it for? What use is it? And the questioner is contented only when given a clear, concise and unambiguous answer that allows the experience to be slotted into a comfortable pre-existing place within the familiar pattern. But old paths only lead to the same old places.

Methodologies

Each of the elements presented in *Tree Breathing* can be used in a variety of ways. They can be can be a meditation tool; a means to attune to tree spirit energies; a divination tool and a method of healing.

Gazing

For meditation and contemplation the words and the symbol for each tree can act as a key to unlock the experience of the tree spirit. The symbol can be a focus for gazing, easily and with relaxed eyes. After a minute or two, simply close the eyes and remain with the experience. With each distraction of thought just return to gazing at the image again for a moment. Keep relaxed with an attitude of openness in your awareness.

Breathing

Whilst gazing at the image imagine that with your in-breath you take in the energy of the symbol. Allow it to fill your body as much as is needed, then relax and sit with the experience. Allow any excess energy to pass through your contact with the ground into the earth.

Doorway Visualisation

Visualise a doorway of some kind in front of you. Place the symbol of the tree on the door. Wait until the door opens and pass through it. Whatever is experienced beyond the threshold is a representation of some aspect of that tree's spirit. Witness or interact as you wish. On returning through the door, give your thanks and make sure that the door is closed. Take a moment to review your experiences before resuming normal activity.

Visualisation

Take the words of the sutra and make internal pictures. Clearly get a feel for the space or environment the words conjure up in you. Enter the picture and interact with what you find. This is a process identical to daydreaming. You just need to keep a little more alert than during ordinary daydreaming so that you do not miss the fine detail and nuance that the deep mind creates with the imagery of the sutra. Allow yourself to move through different stages of creative thought. 'Pretending' is a good way to activate the deep creative processes of the mind. At some point the constructed images will give way to a rapid stream of story sequences, very similar to dreaming, and where practice is needed to maintain enough focus to catch the fleeting imagery without losing yourself and rapidly forgetting them.

Memory, emotion, fears, hopes, wishes will all mingle in these fantasies and it is likely you will find a significant thread or theme that runs through, suggesting how the tree energy may help to balance these issues.

These techniques can be used for experiencing the energy of the tree or for interacting with the tree spirit. All the aforementioned techniques are applicable. It is simply necessary to frame a strong intent before you start that a meaningful interaction with tree or tree spirit is your goal.

Divination/Assessment

As a divinatory method simply focus quietly on the issue and then randomly open the pages. Look at the shape and be aware of any words that might 'jump out' into your awareness from the text. Even if the information is not easy to fathom, using that tree energy will help to resolve the issue that concerns you.

To assess what healing energy is needed a random selection of pages can be used or simply look through the pages until some shape or phrase creates a resonance for you.

As part of a Tree Spirit Healing session, tree breathing can be a powerful element in the sequence of appropriate processes undertaken. The choice of which tree to use will depend upon the methods used. The emotional and mental symphony (or 'symptom picture') that the individual presents may clearly suggest to the healer the usefulness of a certain tree energy over any others. But it is always best to let the deep mind of the client choose the tree energy to work with as there are underlying energy patterns difficult for the conscious awareness to discern. What may appear an obvious priority may not be the safest or most useful place to begin. Using intuitive choice or random selection reveals hidden dynamics, as well as affirming the effectiveness of allowing the deep mind to be heard.

Energy Transference

Working in a healing session with others the energy patterns can be directed from the page to the patient. The simplest method is just to look at the image. The symbol may be visualised inside the patient or it can be transferred in several ways. The first way could be to place one hand over the tree symbol and the other hand on the patient, the energy is then transferred by intention. Alternatively, use the breath to draw in the energy of the tree symbol and then blow it into the person's aura, or into a neutral healing substance that can then be used regularly to encourage healing. Whatever healing method is used, always remember to visualise an open channel into the ground so that inappropriate or excess energies can drain away harmlessly.

Most traditional healing, known from various worldwide shamanic traditions, can be effective templates for using the tools presented here. Other volumes in this series will cover the more particular qualities of each tree. This current book is an opportunity to see the keys and colours for the first time all together. It is hoped that it will provide a helpful resource that can be used by itself, integrated into tree essence therapy or combined with information in other Tree Spirit Healing sourcebooks.

Some Further Thoughts On Tree Spirit Healing
(extracts from *The Tao of Trees*)

Maintaining Balance

A tree does not choose its place of growth. It can only survive and flourish by adjusting its form to harmonise with the prevailing conditions. A tree that grows up, matures, flowers and bears fruit shows that it has succeeded in maintaining that balance for tens, hundreds, even thousands of years. It is this ability to remain balanced and flexible, to absorb and to let go, to remain quiet and harmless, that is transferred to us when we contact the energy of the tree and its spirit.

Meditation Tree

All trees help us towards a meditative state. Tree awareness is always connected to the whole. Tree awareness exists in a cyclical, or spiral, time. Human awareness exists in a linearity of past – present – future. We think at this linear level: evaluating past memory or projecting into the future. The present doesn't hold our attention in the same way. Perception of the present becomes memory or speculation by habit rather than of necessity.

Tree awareness is held in the present, so requires no thought process (or not like ours). When we contact a tree energy we absorb some quality of tree consciousness and so find it easier to release the habitual linearity of thought. This begins to establish a meditative state. (Each tree will have a different quality or 'flavour' depending upon how we interact with its energy.)

Tree awareness is concentric and 360 degrees. Individual awareness is the centre of a circle of energetic liveliness that also includes many other circles of awareness. A tree's individual awareness is not experienced as separate from the circle around it, but as a denser focus of peculiar factors of view and form. The self ("I") cannot have the same meaning where there is no spatial movement or change of view. As humans, we are always in a state of physically changing relationships with our environments. We have therefore to be constantly self-referring to know where we are and what we are doing. A tree exists in one place and has less differentiated parts (organs etc.) so there is not the same need to be self-conscious. More of the awareness can be directed outwards towards the circle's circumference. It is an inclusive awareness rather than a human's exclusive awareness. Entering into tree spirit awareness, we experience a change in metabolism – things slow down, the body relaxes, loses track of its position, sense of time changes, thoughts continue but do not distract us from an underlying, non-verbal vibration of energy, sometimes experienced as bliss or sound or light.

Buddha knew what he was doing sitting under a tree – not just for shade, but for the connection to wholeness of life.

Tree of Voices

We all have the tools necessary for working with tree spirits. The mind and the senses, the body and the emotions have all evolved to be sensitive to the subtle impressions of other life communicating with us. We simply have to rummage around in the bottom of our tool kit to find those specific tools that we have become unfamiliar with through cultural habits.

The spine, the eye, the fingertips are all equally part of the mind. Each message, chemical, electrical, is from one to the other and this extends to our senses, our sense impressions, the world – where all messages, electrical, chemical, sensual web the whole of creation in one great exchange of information and interaction.

For more information see *"Tree: essence, spirit and teacher"*, *"Tree: essence of healing"*, and *"Tree Seer"* by Simon and Sue Lilly, published by Capall Bann, 1999 and 2004. or our websites:

www.greenmantrees.com

www.greenmanshop.co.uk

Alder

oracular stream
fountain head
release

Breath:
In through both ears.
Out through all of the toes.

Apple

sweet sunlight
washing away
completed time

Breath:
In from the distance into the eyes.
Out along arms and legs,
feet and hands.

Ash

cascade equations
flight of anger
cymbals

Breath:
In from the left foot, up the left leg,
to the top of the head.
Out down along the right leg,
into the ground.
(thus making an inverted 'v' shape)

Aspen

shaman's rattle
world's laughter
never mind

Breath:
In, up through the base of the shoulder-blades to the base of the neck. Out, down along the spinal column and from there, spreading out into the peripheral nerves of the body.

Atlas Cedar

rising wood smoke
mountain path
resilience

Breath:
In, up through the soles of the feet.
Out of the centre of the skull
(straight upwards).

Bay

child of suns
victory crown
life blood

Breath:
In through the scalp (across all the top of the head), down to the solar plexus, then the hara, then the pelvis.
Out through all of the skin
(as if radiant light).

Beech

established
enthroned
the clear horizon

Breath:
In, along the ground and up into the lower body, up to the level of the solar plexus.
Out through the centre of the forehead (brow chakra), in a straight line, and also up through the crown of the head (as lines, or crown-shaped, or a ring etc.)

H

Bird Cherry

open
opening
enfolding

Breath:
In through the genitals.
Out through the genitals.

Black Poplar

enfolded
midnight mothers
nurture

Breath:
In, imagining energy concentrating as a column inside the midline of the body. Out, the energy concentrates even more into this central column of energy.

Blackthorn

flowering light
fierce blood
young queen

Breath:
In through the fingertips, up the arms
to the heart.
Out of the heart in a straight line
into the far distance.

Box Tree

drawn to a point
sharp, clear
precise engine

Breath:
In, up through the midline to the centre of the brain.
Out through both nostrils.

Catalpa

heart song
cracked open
fragrance

Breath:
In through the nostrils to the heart.
Out from the heart through both
fingers and toes, into the earth.

Cedar of Lebanon

mountain silent
cloud dance
river racing

Breath:
In through the base of the spine and the genitals.
Out, into the solar plexus concentrating on, and bathing that area.

Cherry Laurel

tuned, acquired
sound signal
gathering together

Breath:
In through the nose and the soft palette
into the skull and brain tissue.
Out through the armpits.

Cherry Plum

light
alighting
unfettered

Breath:
In to the sacral area, (lower abdomen).
Out, down through both the anus and the base of the spine.

Copper Beech

incision of photons
drained doubt
dark before dawn

Breath:
In, from along the ground into the lower body and up to the solar plexus.
Out, down along the arms and fingers into the ground.

Crack Willow

break free
downstream
sunlit ocean

Breath:
In through the palms of the hands
and the fingers.
Out, radiating around the head
like a halo of light.

Douglas Fir

self-sustaining
opening outwards
giant heart

Breath:
In to the diaphragm, base of ribs.
Out, up through the tops
of the shoulders.

Elder

whole heart
all hurt healed
harvest home

Breath:
In through the solar plexus, up into the heart and lungs.
Out through both arms and hands, legs and feet.

English Elm

blue sky
hidden voices
movement of cloud

Breath:
In through the whole surface of the head.
Out, up and out of the whole surface
of the head.

Eucalyptus

rising clear
expansion
cool space

Breath:
In through the base of the diaphragm.
Out through the nostrils (down, to make a circuit of energy with the inbreath).

Field Maple

falling tears
clouds
green shoot sprouts

Breath:
In through the lips.
Out, down all the body.

Fig Tree

cauldron
foundry
forge

Breath:
In through the roof of the mouth (soft palette) to the centre of the brain.
Out, to the centre of the Universe.

Foxglove Tree

downstream
magnificent calm
reflection

Breath:
In through crown of head, simultaneously with first fingers and big toes, to throat. Out through outer corners of eyes (into the distance).

Gean

numberless touch
implacable softness
smoothed cool

Breath:
In through the nose.
Out, diffusing the breath throughout the interior of the body.

Giant Redwood

footprint
heartbeat
wise head

Breath:
In through the soles of each foot, up body,
in two parallel lines.
Out, crossing over at the upper chest
to the other side of body, each line passing
out of body parallel to the ground.

Ginkgo

perfect reflection
inner, outer
ten thousand things

Breath:
In from the universe funnelling into crown of head and down midline to ground.
Out, down and spreading into the ground.

Glastonbury Thorn

unravelling
re-emerging
knitting together

Breath:
In through nose to the heart.
Out from the heart, spiralling outwards
in an anticlockwise direction.

Gorse

lark song
summer sky
weaving together

Breath:
In through the centre of the forehead.
Out through the second and third
fingers of both hands.

Great Sallow

little soul
big earth
holding each other

Breath:
In through the whole of the body surface.
Out through the nostrils.

Hawthorn

warm breath
dark cave
summer stars

Breath:
In, upon a constant stream of moving breeze from the distance in a straight line into the centre of the back (at heart level).
Out, upon the same stream, from the front of the chest.

Hazel

mind depths
bright bubbles
ripples outwards

Breath:
In through the centre of the palms of the hands and the centre of the forehead. Out simultaneously through the throat and the base of the spine.

Holly

power of peace
flowing through
standing firm

Breath:
In through the sides of the ribs,
level with the heart.
Out through the nostrils and the ears.

Holm Oak

holding firm
equilibrium
unperturbed

Breath:
In through both sides of the body,
towards the midline.
Out, crossing at midline and exiting
from opposite sides.

Hornbeam

narrow road
tempered focus
horizon

Breath:
In through the palms of the hands and the centre of the forehead, simultaneously. Out through the centre of the forehead.

Horse Chestnut

silk flame
still cave
seamless time

Breath:
In through the base of the spine
in an anticlockwise spiral, rising
column (pulling in towards midline).
Out through the armpits.

Italian Alder

four winds
sure and safe
quiet room

Breath:
In through the thymus, just above
the heart.
Out through all the toes.

Ivy

heart in light
star in darkness
rope to reach

Breath:
In through all the fingertips to
the heart area.
Out simultaneously through the top
and bottom of the spinal column.

Judas Tree

arising thoughts
weighing mind
abiding sky

Breath:
In through the soles of the feet upwards on the midline of the body.
Out, continuing up and through the top of the head and out into the cosmos.

Juniper

clearing mists
ancient doorway
deep resonance

Breath:
In through the ears, eyes and nose.
Out into the central point of the brain.

Laburnum

fountain head
golden rain
restored, forgiven

Breath:
In through the heart.
Out through the lower abdomen
(sacral chakra).

Larch

delicate touch
senses opening
warp and weft

Breath:
In through the soles of both feet, up the body to the centre of the top of the skull. Out through the outside of the head, along the outside edges of arms and fingers.

Lawson Cypress

sentinel
significator
gnomon

Breath:
In through the entire surface of the skin.
Out through the midline, down into the earth.

Leyland Cypress

what is
is safe
power centre

Breath:
Into the heart.
Out, an expansion outwards from the heart in all directions into the surroundings.

Lilac

antenna
clear channels
pipes of pan

Breath:
In through the base of the spine to
fill up the spinal column.
Out between all the vertebrae at
right angles to the spine.

Lime

dawn light
new path
summer bees

Breath:
Into the heart.
Out through all the body's extremities
(arms,fingers,legs,toes,head,genitals).

Liquidamber

strong passion
silver tongue
sharp eye

Breath:
In through the throat chakra (larynx)
to the heart.
Out through the ears and eyes.

Lombardy Poplar

ignited
expansion
spark upwards

Breath:
In from the ground, through the feet
up the length of the body.
Out through the top of the head, up
into space.

Lucombe Oak

diving through
all possibilities
tasting fullness

Breath:
In through the right side of the head and face.
Out into the lower abdomen,
(hara, sacral chakra).

Magnolia

floating lightly
tremulous wing
laughing fall

Breath:
In, down the midline from the centre of the skull, between the brain's hemispheres, down through the body.
Out, down along the insides of thighs and legs, out of feet into the ground.

Manna Ash

melting
into oneself
happy

Breath:
In, up through the midline to the top of the head.
Out down the same line, into the earth.

Medlar

limitless light
rainbow body
galactic heart

Breath:
In from a point inside the very centre of the body / universe (a conceptual, rather than physical, location) and from there to fill the body.
Out, expanding beyond the body into the universe.

Midland Hawthorn

inner expanse
heart mother
fractal patterns

Breath:
In to the heart.
Out, expanding out from the heart in a sphere. At the outermost edge, there is a sense of the presence of stars.

Mimosa

synaptic elegance
radiant suns
interstices of light

Breath:
In through the fingertips and inside of the thighs to the spine.
Out up the spine, into the cavities, chambers and sinuses of the head.

Monkey Puzzle Tree

invincible view
aeon steps
the smallest sound

Breath:
In to the feet and solar plexus.
Out through the eyes and centre of
forehead into the distance.

Monterey Pine

rock root sinew
resounding deep
bone stirring

Breath:
In through the nostrils, into the brain.
Out through the eyes, into the distance.

Mulberry

distilled
expressed
transfigured

Breath:
In through crown of the head, down to lower abdomen (sacral chakra).
Out through sacral chakra, down to earth.

Norway Maple

gathering in
reinstating
lifting up

Breath:
In to the thymus area (centre of the upper chest).
Out from the thymus area.

Norway Spruce

delight
beacon
axis

Breath:
In through the eyes.
Out through the fingertips.

Oak

firm fixed
flow fast
form finding

Breath:
In, imagining a reciprocal exchange of energy flowing outwards into the world. Out, a reciprocal flow of energy flows into the body so that there is always a perfect balance maintained between the inward and outward flows.

Olive

radiant core
expressed complete
ripened drop

Breath:
In through all the head, (ears, eyes, nose mouth, throat, neck) down into lungs. Out to the sacral chakra then diffusing throughout the inside of the body.

Osier

air rooted
earth rooted
spirit rooted

Breath:
In through the anus.
Out through the eyes.

Pear

reflections woven
ascension song
molecular dance

Breath:
In through the nipples.
Out through the pelvic floor towards the centre of the earth.

Persian Ironwood

iron
anchor
i am

Breath:
In simultaneously through the throat chakra and palms of the hands.
Out simultaneously through the soles of the feet (downwards) and up through the crown of the head.

Pittospora

choosing neither
take one
leave regret

Breath:
In through the left nostril.
Out through the right nostril.

Plane Tree

spiral rising
falcon's eye
diadem

Breath:
In through the brow (Ajna chakra) to the heart, then solar plexus.
Out from solar plexus to palms of hands (and outwards).

Plum

fruit of flesh
flesh of fruit
fire power

Breath:
In, to the sacral area (lower abdomen).
Out, focusing even more tightly into the sacral centre.

Privet

pierced, broken
river of life
unperturbed

Breath:
In from soles of feet, filling up entire inside of body to top of head.
Out as if emptying back down from head to feet.

Red Chestnut

let go
go on
falling safely

Breath:
In to the crown of the head, down the body's midline.
Out down the arms and legs, out of fingertips and toes.

Red Oak

kindle clearly
bones and roots
heart fires

Breath:
In up into the balls of the feet,
concentrate there as spinning energy.
Out, unwinding back down into the earth.

Robinia

clear window
transparent mind
tranquil gaze

Breath:
In through nostrils down to lungs,
then to all organs of body.
Out into the brain, then outwards.

Rowan

star and stone
voice shapes space
big mind singing

Breath:
In, visualising yourself within a waterfall of energy from the stars overhead, flowing around your body.
Out continuing the same flow downwards into the earth.

Scots Pine

glimmer spark
horizon of seeing
illumination!

Breath:
In through the tip of the tongue (keep mouth slightly open, tongue not touching). Out through the centre of the eyes, straight into the distance).

Sea Buckthorn

sea breeze
salt foam
the road inland

Breath:
In from the ground, or from the space between your feet and the ground, into your feet.
Out from your feet, making a continuous cycle of revolving air, as if floating or hovering.

Sequoia

valley spirit
gateway
heaven and earth

Breath:
In through the bones of the feet,
up through all the bones of the body.
Out, allowing the breath to relax and
collect within the pelvic cavity.

Silver Birch

bone white
birth reveals
all in beauty

Breath:
In through the solar plexus.
Out, swirling around the inner sides of the body walls, (as liquid swirls around a vessel).

Silver Fir

enthroned
open crown
starlight descent

Breath:
In from centre of the earth, up midline
to just above the top of the head.
Out, into, and concentrating in, the area
just below the diaphragm / ribcage.

Silver Maple

life streams
body weather
mood tides

Breath:
In through the nose and roof of mouth
to centre of the brain.
Out through all the blood vessels to
extremities and downwards.

Spindle

sudden bright sun
clarity of edge
revealing darkness

Breath:
In as a thin, blade-like line of light from the centre of the skull down into the body. Out, the line opens, like a fan, so that the light spreads out illuminating body and aura.

Stag's Horn Sumach

mind pool
ripple thoughts
translucence

Breath:
In through all the sense organs of head,
(ears, eyes, nose, tongue, skin).
Out down the midline of the body,
deep into the earth.

Strawberry Tree

suspension
submerge
silence

Breath:
In through the wrist pulses (both sides).
Out through the wrist pulses.

Sweet Chestnut

single thread
untangled
present moment

Breath:
In from the ground up the midline of the body.
Out in a V-shape down both legs into the ground.

Sycamore

sweetness
warm belly
deep smile

Breath:
In through the centre of the palms of hands and soles of feet to solar plexus. Out, downwards from the pelvis and legs.

Tamarisk

offering up
phoenix fire
alchemical gold

Breath:
In, drawing down from above the head in an anti-clockwise spiral vortex, around and into the body.
Out, in a clockwise spiral vortex into the earth.
The next breath reverses this flow, (clockwise up into body, out into cosmos; anticlockwise down into earth). Repeat.

Tree Lichen

heaven whispers
zephyrs
fountains

Breath:
In to the head and upper torso / chest.
Out, into the centre of one's being
(a conceptual, non-localised point).

Tree of Heaven

flowering upwards
new view
soles of the feet

Breath:
In through the sacral chakra
(lower abdomen).
Out, down into the lower pelvic area
(centre of gravity).

Tulip Tree

one full moment
then another
poised repose

Breath:
In, up the midline and branching out into the body.
Out, extending those energy lines upwards and outwards.

Viburnum

heart haven
healing spirit
just ask

Breath:
In from the extremities of the body
to the heart.
Out from the heart to the extremities
of the body.

Walnut

mirror-bright
smoke screen
inviolable

Breath:
In through the soles of the feet,
up the legs.
Out through the eyes and palms of hands
(that are held up and facing outwards).

Wayfaring Tree

circular paths
old songs
falling awake

Breath:
In through the crown of the head, swirling around the brain and skull.
Out through the outer corners of the eyes.

Weeping Willow

water's edge
surface tension
sun dancing

Breath:
In through the base of the spine (root chakra) and up to the solar plexus.
Out from the solar plexus.

Western Hemlock

mountain continues
horizon remains
open grace

Breath:
In through the crown of the head, down to the solar plexus.
Out through the solar plexus.

Western Red Cedar

beneath the waters
constant peace
tidal constant

Breath:
In through the centre of the forehead.
Out through the nostrils.

Whitebeam

heart's eye
transparency
other worlds

Breath:
In through the whole of the surface
of the skin (all over the body).
Out through the whole of the skin.

White Poplar

turn around
light, dark
dancing

Breath:
In through the toes and feet, keeping the breath in that area.
Out through the toes and feet, as if rooting into the ground.

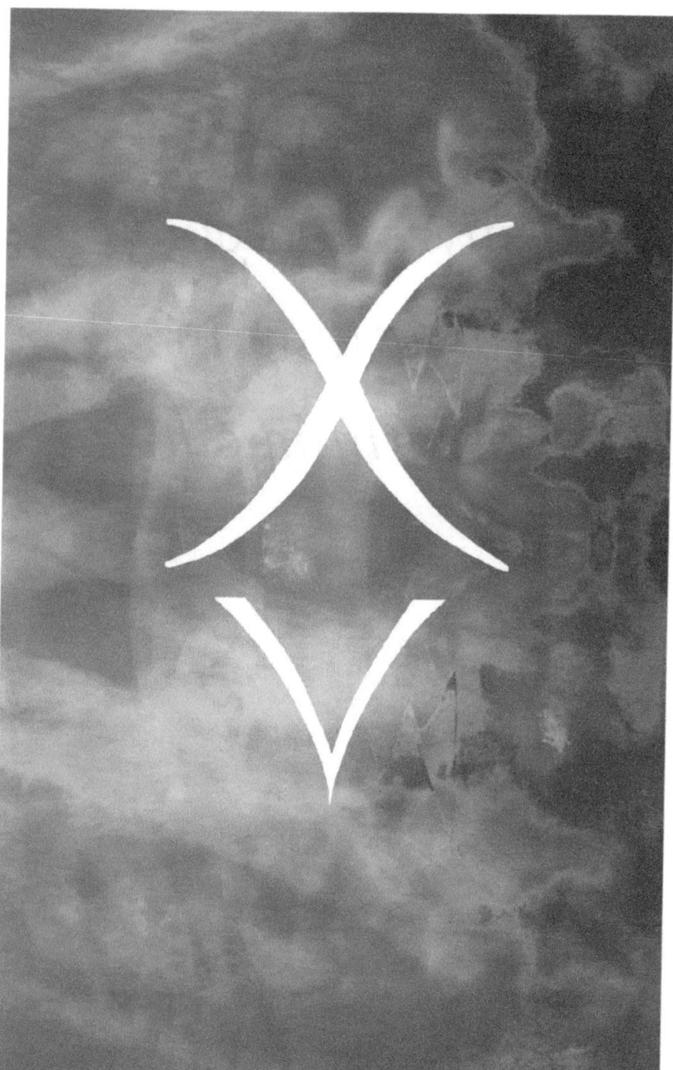

White Willow

silver and gold
breathing in
breathing out

Breath:
In through the palms of the hands
and the fingers.
Out, radiating from the head
(as if a halo).

Wild Service Tree

graciously remaining
dreaming tree
complete

Breath:
In to the solar plexus and the diaphragm.
Out through the crown of the head.

Willow-leaved Pear

serene centre
slow leap
long arc

Breath:
In through the base of the spine, up
into solar plexus, then filling abdomen.
Out, up through the spinal column
from top of head into cosmos.

Wych Elm

attainment of realms
rest secure
clear peace

Breath:
In through the scalp / crown of head.
Out from the throat chakra.
(Then alternate these with each breath).

Yellow Buckeye

shining one
illuminated one
accommodation

Breath:
In through centres of the palms
of hands and nostrils simultaneously.
Out from eyes and heart simultaneously.

Yew

infrasound
stirring
healing poison

Breath:
In, imagining a vortex pulled down from above head on midline, pushing deep into the earth.
Out, expanding out from body in a widening circle into the world.

blurb